Colonial America

An Interactive History Adventure

by Allison Lassieur

Consultant:
Len Travers
Associate Professor of History
University of Massachusetts at Dartmouth

CAPSTONE PRESS
a capstone imprint

You Choose Books are published by Capstone Press,
1710 Roe Crest Drive, North Mankato, Minnesota 56003
www.capstonepub.com

Books published by Capstone Press are manufactured with paper
containing at least 10 percent post-consumer waste.

Library of Congress Cataloging-in-Publication Data
Lassieur, Allison.
  Colonial America : an interactive history adventure / by Allison Lassieur.
      p. cm. — (You choose—historical eras)
  Summary:"Describes the people and events involved during the colonial years before the
Revolutionary War. The reader's choices reveal the historical details from the perspectives of an
indentured Virginia servant, a Massachusetts colonist, and a resident of Philadelphia just before
the revolution"—Provided by publisher.
  Includes bibliographical references and index.
  ISBN 978-1-4296-5481-4 (library binding) — ISBN 978-1-4296-6277-2 (paperback)
  1. United States—History—Colonial period, ca. 1600–1775—Juvenile literature. 2. United
States—Social life and customs—To 1775—Juvenile literature. I. Title. II. Series.
  E188.L367 2011
  973.2—dc22   2010035013

Editorial Credits
Angie Kaelberer, editor; Bobbie Nuytten, designer; Wanda Winch, media researcher;
    Eric Manske, production specialist

Photo Credits
Alamy: North Wind Picture Archives, cover, 10, 44, 68, 74; The Bridgeman Art Library
International: Courtesy of Historical Society of Pennsylvania Collection/Atwater Kent Museum
of Philadelphia/ Clyde Osmer Deland, 91, ©Look and Learn/Private Collection, 14, ©Look
and Learn/Private Collection/Peter Jackson, 12, ©Look and Learn/Private Collection/Ron
Embleton, 59, Peter Newark American Pictures, 53, Worcester Art Museum, Massachusetts,
USA/Willem van de Velde, the younger, 20, Yale Center for British Art, Paul Mellon Collection,
USA/Sir Joshua Reynolds, 57; Corbis: Bettmann, 99, Freelance Photography Guild, 81, Photo
Images/Lee Snider, 72; Getty Images: Hulton Archive, 83; The Granger Collection, 103;
National Geographic Stock: Louis S. Glanzman, 43; National Parks Service/Colonial National
Historical Park, 6, 29, 100; SuperStock Inc.: SuperStock, 24

Printed in the United States of America in Stevens Point, Wisconsin.
072013   007623R

TABLE OF CONTENTS

ABOUT YOUR ADVENTURE

YOU are living in America during colonial times. Thousands of people have left Europe to settle the vast lands in North America. Will they stay loyal to their home countries, or will they break away to form a country of their own?

In this book you'll explore how the choices people made meant the difference between life and death. The events you'll experience happened to real people.

Chapter One sets the scene. Then you choose which path to read. Follow the directions at the bottom of each page. The choices you make will change your outcome. After you finish your path, go back and read the others for new perspectives and more adventures.

YOU CHOOSE the path
you take through history.

Colonists landed in
Jamestown, Virginia,
in 1607.

A Time of Change

Ever since the first settlers landed in Virginia in 1607, the American colonies have been a part of Great Britain. Most people came to the colonies from Europe in search of better lives. Some came to the colonies to start businesses or farms. Others came as servants for wealthy people who paid for their trip across the Atlantic. Still others weren't there by choice. They were kidnapped in Africa and brought to the colonies as slaves.

Turn the page.

The colonies grew quickly. There were three main areas—the southern colonies, the middle colonies, and the New England colonies.

In the southern colonies, the warm climate and good soil allowed people to build large plantations and farms. They raised tobacco, cotton, and rice. In the middle colonies, farmers grew wheat, and industries such as shipbuilding and ironworks began. The soil in the New England colonies was too rocky for large farms, but rich forests provided timber and furs. The oceans near New England teemed with fish. Towns such as Boston and Philadelphia grew to cities of thousands of people.

(part of Massachusetts)

N.H.

Lake Champlain
Fort Ticonderoga

Marblehead
Mass. • Boston

Conn.
R.I.

Hudson R.

New York

Pennsylvania
Philadelphia • New Jersey

Maryland
Delaware

St. Mary's City •

Virginia

Chesapeake Bay

Jamestown

North Carolina

South Carolina

Georgia

Atlantic Ocean

New England Colonies
Middle Colonies
Southern Colonies

N

| 0 | 100 | 200 miles |
| 0 | 100 | 200 kilometers |

9

Turn the page.

Many colonists were upset about paying taxes to the British.

In the 1700s the British fought several wars in the colonies, including the French and Indian War. Most colonists were still loyal to Britain and gladly fought in the British Army. These wars were expensive, though. The British Parliament began to tax the colonies to raise money.

Many colonists thought the new taxes were unfair. They believed they should have some say in Britain's government if they were expected to pay British taxes. But the British didn't want to give the colonies more freedom. By the late 1700s, the colonies had enough. They began to fight back.

What will your experience in colonial America be like?

→ To experience life as an indentured servant in Virginia in 1645, turn to page **13**.

→ To discover colonial life in Massachusetts in 1759, turn to page **45**.

→ To live in colonial Philadelphia right before the Revolutionary War, turn to page **75**.

The streets of London were full of beggars in the mid-1600s.

CHAPTER 2

A New Life in the Colonies

It's early afternoon in London, England. You stumble down the narrow cobblestone streets that stink of garbage and human waste. It's 1645, and like thousands of other people in England, you're out of work. But no one is hiring right now.

You reach into your pocket and feel the coins there. Not many left. You see the open door of a coaching inn called The George. At coaching inns drivers and others can get a cheap, hot meal. The place is empty except for a large man behind the bar.

Turn the page.

People became indentured servants to pay their ship fare to the colonies.

"Looking for work, miss?" the man says, kindly handing you a crust of bread and mug of ale. You nod, your mouth full.

"Your best chance is to go to the colonies," the man says. "There's work there and land and riches for anyone willing to work hard."

"I wish I could, but I can't afford the ship fare," you reply.

"You can agree to work as an indentured servant in exchange for the cost of your voyage," the man explains. "When your term of service is done, you're free to do as you please."

That sounds too good to be true. "What must I do to get passage on one of these ships?"

The man replies, "One way is to sign a contract with an agent. He finds servants for wealthy landowners. Or you can sign a contract with a ship's captain. He'll sell your contract to someone once you reach the colonies."

→ To find an agent, turn to page **16**.

→ To take your chances with a ship's captain, turn to page **17**.

The bartender tells you where to find an agent. Soon you are standing before a tall, well-dressed man.

"I am Philip Smith, and I'm looking for servants to go to Virginia," the man says. "Do you have any skills?"

"I'm very good with a needle, sir," you say. The man nods his head. "Sign this paper. It says that in exchange for the cost of your voyage, you agree to work for four years. You'll receive room, board, and a new set of clothing once a year. When your term of service is finished, you'll receive land for your dowry, a new set of clothing, and some money."

Excitedly, you sign. Smith hands you a copy of the contract. "The ship leaves tomorrow at noon," he says. "Don't be late."

➤ *Turn to page 19.*

The next morning you make your way to the docks. A sailor points out a captain who's looking for passengers to the colonies.

"I'm strong and I can sew well," you say.

"Very well," the captain says. He hands you a paper to sign and motions for you to board his ship. "We'll be leaving this afternoon."

You climb aboard and find a corner in a cabin. The voyage lasts two months. By that time you are dirty and tired of sleeping in the cramped, smelly cabin. One day you see land. You've reached Virginia!

When the ship lands, everyone spills out onto the dock. One by one the captain calls each person's name. Then he sells the person's indenture contract. When your name is called, you slowly walk forward.

Turn the page.

"This gentleman is a representative of Governor William Berkeley," the captain says, introducing a well-dressed man. "The governor has need for a maid."

You agree to become a servant in the governor's household. The gentleman pays the captain for your contract and tells you to follow him to a waiting wagon.

"I am Charles," the man says. "The governor owns a large plantation in the country. He also has a house in Jamestown. He needs a maid for both houses."

➤ *To live on the plantation, turn to page* **21**.

➤ *To live in Jamestown, turn to page* **28**.

By midmorning you're already at the docks, scanning the crowds for a sign of Smith. When he sees you, he waves.

"Welcome," he says. "I'm glad you decided to come."

You walk up the wooden planking to the deck of the ship. It's covered with crates of flour, dried meats, dried beans, and other foods for the voyage. Below the decks are a few passenger cabins. They're crowded, but you manage to find a small cot.

The ship begins to move away from the dock, making your stomach lurch. You hope the sick feeling will pass.

You spend most of the next few days on the deck. The cool sea air there makes your seasickness better. One afternoon the sky turns black. Large waves bash against the ship.

Turn the page.

"Get below deck," the captain shouts. "This looks to be a bad storm."

You know you should obey, but you hate being in the dark, smelly space below the deck.

Settlers sailing to America often faced raging storms at sea.

→ *To go below, turn to page 34.*

→ *To stay on deck, turn to page 35.*

The Virginia countryside is lush and green, with thick forests. After a long ride, you arrive at Green Spring plantation. The elegant brick mansion is surrounded by a large barn and several outbuildings.

Groups of workers toil in the tobacco fields beyond the house. You're surprised to see a few black men among the workers. You've never seen a black person before.

"Who are those men with dark skin?" you ask Charles.

"They're servants from Africa," he replies. "Like you, they also work without pay. But some of them may never be free."

Never to be free! That is hard to imagine.

Turn the page.

At the house a middle-aged woman named Mary greets you. She shows you to a small room upstairs. "Here, put this on," Mary says, handing you a clean dress and apron. "You'll get a new set of clothing every year, including shoes," she says. "The governor is good to his servants. I served my indenture five years ago, but I stayed on as a freewoman."

After you change you go downstairs, marveling at the gleaming wood floors and the fine furniture. Mary is in the kitchen.

"There's much to do," she says, stirring a large pot hanging over the fire. "Either go draw water from the spring, or busy yourself with cleaning the governor's study."

➤ To get water, go to page **23**.

➤ To clean the study, turn to page **24**.

You're out the door before you realize that you don't know where the spring is. A handsome young man approaches you.

"I'm James. You must be the new house maid."

You nod. "I'm supposed to get water."

"I'll take you to the spring," he says. James leads you to a mossy spring. You fill the buckets and turn toward the house. James tells you that he is also an indentured servant from London.

"When I am free, I will get a piece of land for my own," he says proudly. He winks and says, "And by then I'll need a pretty wife." You duck into the kitchen before he can see you blushing.

→ *Turn to page 26.*

William Berkeley served as governor of Virginia for 28 years.

A dignified man in a long, curly wig rises from a chair when you enter. "I'm William Berkeley," the man says with a smile. "You must be my new servant. Welcome to Green Spring."

You curtsy, astonished that such a great man would be kind to a lowly servant. The governor sits down and returns to the letter he was writing. Quietly you move about the room as you clean. The governor's silk frock coat is hanging on the back of a chair. It has a large tear in the sleeve.

"Excuse me, sir," you say, "I can repair this."

Governor Berkeley looks up from his letter. "Are you skilled with a needle?" he asks.

"Yes, sir," you reply proudly. "I can sew anything, and I can mend so well that you'll never know it was torn."

"Very well then," he says. "I expect it to be finished by morning."

As you slip out the door, you almost run into a tall young man. "Hello there," he says to you. "My name is James. Are you the new maid?"

You nod. James tells you he's also an indentured servant from London. "I'm sure we'll see a lot of each other around here," he calls after you as you hurry back to the kitchen.

➤ *Turn the page.*

Your skill as a seamstress is immediately put to use. Soon you are sewing clothing, sheets, towels, linens, and anything else that is needed.

James has been courting you since you arrived. Two years after your arrival, he finishes his indenture. He asks you to marry him. "I've been given 50 acres of land a few miles from here," he says. "I can use the money I also received to buy out your indenture. If the governor gives you permission to marry me, we can start a life of freedom together."

You're not sure if you want to marry James. Clearing farmland is backbreaking work. You could continue living here as a freewoman, like Mary, once your term of service is up.

→ To marry James, go to page **27**.

→ To stay at Green Spring, turn to page **36**.

The governor gives his permission for the marriage. He agrees to let James buy the remainder of your indenture.

James builds a small cabin on the land he received. You begin to clear land for a tobacco crop. It's hard work, but you are too poor to buy an indentured servant or to hire a free person to help. There are days when it seems you made the wrong choice. But you own land. That's far more than you could have hoped for in London.

One afternoon you are outside gathering firewood. Something rustles in the trees. You turn and see a dark face looking back at you. The man's eyes are full of fear. "Please help me," he rasps in a hoarse voice.

➺ *To refuse to help, turn to page 37.*

➺ *To help the man, turn to page 38.*

The streets of Jamestown are lined with well-kept homes. One is a large brick house that stands high above the smaller wooden buildings. To your surprise, the wagon pulls up to this house.

"This is the only brick house in Jamestown," Charles says. "It was built by Richard Kemp, the former secretary of the Virginia Colony. Governor Berkeley owns it now. He stays mainly at Green Spring plantation. Mistress Constance oversees this house."

A tall, stern woman opens the door. "Get in here," she snaps at you. "I don't have time for lazy servants."

You're tired from your journey, but you obediently follow Mistress Constance inside. She leads you up a set of narrow stairs to the second floor, which is little more than an attic.

Governor Berkeley lived in a Jamestown house similar to this one.

"This is where you'll sleep," she says. "Now, change out of that filthy dress. I won't have my servants looking like beggars."

Turn the page.

You drop your small bundle of possessions and change into your other dress. When you get downstairs, Mistress Constance is in the kitchen, barking orders to two other servants. Soon you are busily working to prepare the evening meal. It is late before the kitchen is clean, and the fires are banked for the night. All you're given to eat is a crust of bread and a bowl of burned stew, but you gulp it hungrily.

Finally you climb the stairs and collapse in your corner of the attic. "What have I done?" you think to yourself as you fall asleep.

The next few months are a blur of hard work and hunger. You are overwhelmed with mending and sewing for the whole household. The only food you get is a weak gruel, bread, and water.

One afternoon you are sewing outside when a young woman approaches you.

"It's a shame that Mistress Constance treats you so badly. If you lived with my mistress, she would treat you much better," she says.

Surprised, you look up at the woman. "Whom do you work for?"

"Mistress Margaret Brent, in Maryland," the servant replies. "She owns a huge plantation and is very kind. My name is Jane. Mistress Brent is here visiting, and I came with her."

"Do you think she would buy my contract?" you ask Jane.

Turn the page.

Jane bends down and whispers, "If you can make your way to the plantation, I'm sure she will give you a good home in exchange for three years of service. The farm is outside St. Mary's City, Maryland. It is called Sister's Freehold."

Run away! Indentured servants disappear all the time. But if you're caught, you could have years added to your term of service.

➤ To run away, go to page **33**.

➤ To stay, turn to page **40**.

The next night you wrap your belongings in a bundle and creep downstairs. You take half a loaf of bread and some dried meat from the kitchen.

For the next several weeks you make your way slowly to Maryland. You sleep by day and travel at night. Your food soon runs out. You forage in the woods for berries and steal food from the few homesteads along the way. A kind boat captain agrees to give you a ride across the Chesapeake Bay. Finally, exhausted and nearly starving, you arrive at St. Mary's City. Suddenly you have a thought. No one here knows you. If people think you are a freewoman, you could get a job and be free for good.

➤ *To stay in town, turn to page* **41**.

➤ *To go to the plantation, turn to page* **42**.

Reluctantly you go below. The ship tosses and lurches in the storm. You vomit several times. The storm is over quickly, but you still feel sick. Maybe if you sleep for a time, you'll feel better.

But the sickness gets worse. Sores form on your tongue, followed by red, raised bumps on your hands and face. It's smallpox! This disease is very contagious. No one will come near you. After two more days of suffering you die, never seeing the colonies.

34

THE END

To follow another path, turn to page 11.
To read the conclusion, turn to page 101.

When the captain isn't looking, you hide behind a stack of wooden crates. Huge waves crash over the deck, soaking you with icy ocean water. Sailors run back and forth, making sure everything on deck is secured. The captain yells orders over the roar of the storm.

As you huddle on deck, you notice that one of the ropes holding the crates is loose. It might be wise to find another hiding place. You get up just as a huge wave throws you into the stack of crates. They tumble down on top of you, crushing you instantly. Then they slide into the wild ocean, taking your body with them.

35

THE END

To follow another path, turn to page 11.
To read the conclusion, turn to page 101.

"I'm quite fond of you, James," you say. "But I am content to stay here. I'm sure you'll find another girl who will make you a good wife."

James leaves, but you don't regret your decision. You're not ready to marry. You don't want to give up all your rights to a husband, which is the law.

Life on the plantation is filled with hard work, but you're treated fairly. When your term of indenture is over, the governor agrees to let you stay on as a paid servant. Mary recently died of a fever, so you become the head maid. You oversee the servants and make sure the house runs smoothly. Life is good, and you are content to stay here forever.

THE END

To follow another path, turn to page 11.
To read the conclusion, turn to page 101.

The black man must be a runaway servant. You know the punishment for helping runaways can be harsh.

"No, I cannot help you," you tell the man. "You need to leave here now!"

The man turns and runs back into the forest. A few days later, you hear that the man was caught nearby. He received a severe whipping as punishment and nearly died. Plus, he'll never earn his freedom. You feel guilty about not helping him. You decide that if another runaway shows up at your door, you will help however you can.

37

THE END

To follow another path, turn to page 11.
To read the conclusion, turn to page 101.

It wasn't that long ago that you were in a similar situation as this man. You were treated well, but that is not the case for everyone.

"Quick, come inside," you tell the black man. James is hunting, but he'll be back soon. You don't think he'd approve of you helping a runaway.

"Why are you running away?" you ask the man as you hand him a slice of corn bread and a cup of water.

"My master whipped me for falling asleep in the fields," he replies. He lifts the back of his ragged shirt. You're horrified to see bloody welts on his back. You quickly mix up a poultice for the man's wounds. "This should help the pain and prevent an infection," you tell him.

"Thank you," the man says. "I need to be going now—I can't put you in any more danger."

You send the man away with a few more slices of corn bread and some bacon. As he slips into the forest, you realize that you never asked his name. That's probably best. The less you know, the less you'll be able to tell anyone who comes looking for him. With a sigh, you start making supper. You usually share everything with James, but you'll keep this story to yourself.

THE END

To follow another path, turn to page 11.
To read the conclusion, turn to page 101.

As much as you hate this place, you don't want to risk being beaten for running away. Governor Berkeley seems kind enough when he visits the house, but you don't know him. He could easily hire someone to track you down. Perhaps if you work harder, Mistress Constance will be kinder to you. You have three years left on your contract, and then you'll be free forever.

THE END

To follow another path, turn to page 11.
To read the conclusion, turn to page 101.

As you walk through town, you see houses being built and others repaired. A passerby tells you that the town recently came under attack. An Englishman named Richard Ingle and his followers took over the colony's government. The governor, Leonard Calvert, fled to Virginia.

Calvert is now back in power, but the town is still recovering. There is a need for craftspeople with good skills. People start hiring you to mend and wash their clothes. Soon you have enough money to rent a small building in town. You're happy to have your own business and most of all, your freedom.

THE END

To follow another path, turn to page 11.
To read the conclusion, turn to page 101.

Everyone knows where Sister's Freehold plantation is, so you have no trouble finding it. When you knock on the door, Jane answers.

"I'm so glad you came!" she cries. She leads you through the house to a sunny room where Mistress Margaret is sitting.

"Mistress, this is the girl I told you about," Jane says, nudging you forward. You curtsy shyly.

"Welcome to Maryland," Mistress Margaret says. "I don't want to know where you came from, do you understand? Giving shelter to a fugitive servant is against the law."

You nod, and Mistress Margaret smiles. "Very well, I'm glad you're here." You are given a small room of your own. Soon you are busy mending and sewing for Mistress Margaret and the rest of the household.

You're surprised to learn that Mistress Margaret isn't married. She owns the plantation with her sister, Mary. Both sisters treat you well. The terrible experiences in Jamestown fade from your memory as you settle into life in Maryland.

Margaret Brent asked for the right to vote in the Maryland Assembly.

THE END

To follow another path, turn to page 11.
To read the conclusion, turn to page 101.

Many settlers came to the colonies hoping to own land.

CHAPTER 3

To Sea or To War?

Leaning against your hoe, you gaze out onto the field you're weeding. Beyond the field, the woods stretch for miles.

You've lived on this small Massachusetts farm all your life. Before you were born, your mother and father came to the colonies from England. They hoped to own land and have the freedom to live however they chose.

45

Turn the page.

Now it is 1759, and the farm is doing well. Your family includes you and two older brothers. Adam, the oldest, loves the farm and wants to stay here forever. He will inherit it from your father one day. Your middle brother, Jeremiah, left to become a fisherman. Now he lives in Marblehead, Massachusetts, a large fishing town on the coast.

But you're the youngest son. You won't inherit any land, and you're not sure what you'll do with your life.

You see a horse and rider coming toward the farm. It's Jeremiah!

Soon you are all around the table, eating the noon meal of beans and fresh bread. When the meal is done, Mother clears the wooden plates from the table. Father, Adam, and Jeremiah light their pipes.

"I'm hearing much about the French and Indian War that's going on," Father says. "A Massachusetts militia is forming to fight the French in the north. As a member of our local militia, I'm thinking about joining them."

Jeremiah snorts, "I don't like the French, but I don't want to kill them. I'm staying in Marblehead." He looks at you. "My skipper could use a strong young man like you," he says. "How would you like to become a fisherman?"

Before you have time to say anything, Father looks at you. "You know how to handle a musket. You would make a fine soldier for Britain."

47

➤ *To go with Jeremiah, turn to page 48.*

➤ *To become a soldier, turn to page 54.*

Jeremiah entertains you with tales of life on a fishing boat during the ride to Marblehead. At the docks, he introduces you to Skipper John Bridges of the schooner *Rebecca Bay*. The skipper looks at you warily.

"You start as a cuttail," he says. "You'll cut bait, bait hooks, and process the catch. You'll be paid five shillings, plus your food, and a penny for every fish you catch." That sounds like a huge sum to you, so you nod eagerly.

"We leave tomorrow. Be here at dawn or we'll sail without you."

Jeremiah says, "I usually sleep on board the night before we leave. But today is your first day as a fisherman. Shall we celebrate in town?"

→ *To stay on the boat, go to page* **49**.

→ *To celebrate, turn to page* **62**.

As much as you'd like to visit a tavern, it's better to be ready when the ship leaves. Jeremiah introduces you to the other seven men on the ship. Two of them, Daniel and Jeb, are cuttails like you. The others are sharesmen, like Jeremiah. Sharesmen do most of the catching and earn a share of the profits. Skipper John chooses the fishing location and keeps count of the fish caught.

The ship sails out of port at sunrise. It's a 10-day journey to the cod fishing grounds. Daniel and Jeb show you how to cut mackerel and clams into bait.

Finally Skipper John drops anchor. You and the other cuttails bait the hooks. You attach the hooks to long lines weighted with lead. The sharesmen throw the lines into the water. When fish take the bait, the sharesmen haul them up to the deck and throw them into a container.

Turn the page.

Baiting the hooks is boring. You want to catch a fish. When you ask Jeremiah, he laughs. "Your job is baiting," he says. "You'll move on to catching when you're ready."

You see a line bobbing in the water. A fish has taken the bait. Everyone else is busy with other lines. Now is your chance.

→ To call for help, go to page 51.

→ To haul up the fish, turn to page 64.

"There's a big one here!" you cry. Jeremiah soon hauls up the biggest fish you've ever seen. It must weigh at least 50 pounds! You make a notch in its tail to show that you helped catch it.

After a few hours, the container is filled with fish. The men split the fish open and pull out the guts. They then cut off the heads and tails and remove the spines. You carefully remove each cod's liver, which is used to make oil for lamps. The waste is thrown into buckets to be used as bait for the next catch.

As you reach into a fish to cut out the liver, the ship lurches. The knife slices deeply into your hand. Quickly Jeremiah wraps a cloth around your hand to stop the bleeding.

➤ To report the cut to the skipper, turn to page **52**.

➤ To ignore the cut, turn to page **65**.

Skipper John takes one look at the wound and tells you to stop working. "We've got to get you back to port," he says. The others finish processing the fish as the skipper turns the ship toward home.

You're starting to feel feverish, which is a sign that the wound is infected. When the ship reaches Marblehead, the skipper finds a doctor. He cleans the wound, pulling out clots of dead, infected flesh. Then he heats up an iron rod and cauterizes the wound. You pass out from the pain. But when you wake up, you feel better.

You rest at a tavern for several days. One morning you wake up feeling stronger. You walk to the docks to find Skipper John.

"How's the hand?" he asks.

You show him the scar. "Thank you," you say. "You saved my life."

"We're going back out tomorrow," Skipper John says gruffly. "Can I count on you as one of my crew?"

You'd like to stay. But you just received a letter from your oldest brother, Adam. Father has joined the militia fighting the war. Adam needs help on the farm.

Dried codfish was one of the main products of the New England colonies.

→ To go back to sea, turn to page **66**.

→ To go home, turn to page **67**.

You tell Jeremiah good-bye. Then you and Father go to meet other Massachusetts men at a local inn. The group soon sets out northwest toward New York.

"What is this war all about, anyway?" your 16-year-old neighbor Seth asks.

"The French are trying to take our land," Father tells him. "Many Indian tribes have sided with the French against us. That's why we've been called to fight with our fellow British."

By the time you reach the New York border, your group numbers more than 100. There is talk of Indian attacks in the area, so you take turns keeping watch at night.

One night it's your turn. You're sitting against a tree when you hear a faint rustle in the woods.

➤ To go for help, go to page 55.

➤ To investigate the sound, turn to page 68.

"There's someone in the woods!" you shout, waking your father and several other men. They jump up and join you as you run into the woods. Several figures are slipping through the shadows, but they're moving too fast to chase.

"Must have been Indians," Father says. "Good thing you were on watch." You smile proudly.

In late June your group arrives at the south end of Lake George, where the British Army has gathered. Thousands of men must be here! As you set up camp, two men stride up to Father.

"Are you Massachusetts men?" one man asks. "I am General Timothy Ruggles, commander of the Massachusetts forces. Welcome!"

"And I am your commander, Major General Jeffrey Amherst," the second man says coolly.

Turn the page.

As they leave, Father whispers, "Lord Amherst doesn't like us colonists, but he's a good leader. He wants to capture Fort Carillon, a French fort on Lake Champlain."

"Where's Lake Champlain?" you ask.

"It's just north of here," Father explains. "Lake George flows into Lake Champlain."

For weeks you and the other soldiers march, drill, shoot target practice, and prepare the cannons. Ships ferry cannons and soldiers across Lake George. Finally everything is in place.

The evening of July 25, a stranger appears at your campfire. He has an air of confidence about him like an officer. He smiles at you.

"I'm Robert Rogers," the man says. "I hear you have sharp eyes and a steady hand. I'm in need of men such as you."

Jeffrey Amherst led the British Army against the French.

You've heard of Rogers and his force, Rogers' Rangers. They are famous for being excellent soldiers and performing sneak attacks. But their missions are usually very dangerous.

"The general has given us a mission," he continues. "If we succeed we are guaranteed to defeat the French."

➤ To stay with the Massachusetts regiment, turn to page **58**.

➤ To join Rogers' Rangers, turn to page **59**.

"Thank you, but I want to fight with my fellow Massachusetts soldiers," you say. Rogers nods, shakes your hand, and disappears into the darkness. You can't believe that you were asked to become a Ranger, but you made the right choice.

General Ruggles walks by and sees you by the fire. "Ready for battle?" he asks kindly. You nod, hoping that you don't look as nervous as you feel.

"Don't worry," he says. "We can fight better than the French." The general walks away as you crawl into the tent you share with your father. You settle into an uneasy sleep.

➼ Turn to page 71.

There's no way you will turn down such an offer. You find Father and tell him. He claps your back proudly. "Be safe," he says.

You follow Rogers to the Rangers' camp, where about 60 men are gathered.

Rogers' Rangers were known for their fighting skills and bravery.

Turn the page.

"The French have set a trap in the lake," Rogers says. "It's a line of logs chained together, called a boom. It stretches across the lake behind the fort and will block our boats from getting close to the fort. We need to destroy the boom."

Rogers leads the group to the shore. A line of boats bobs in the water. Quietly you and the men climb into the boats and row toward the fort. Each boat carries several large saws.

"Be careful," Rogers calls softly. "The French have cannons on the shore." When you get to the boom, most of the men slip into the lake and begin sawing the logs. You can join them, or you can stay in the boat and watch for enemies.

➤ *To stay in the boat, go to page 61.*

➤ *To cut the logs, turn to page 69.*

You and several others keep watch, but the French never appear. Some of the other Rangers row quietly to the eastern shore. They set up a few tents and build a campfire.

"What are they doing?" you hiss. "They'll be seen!"

"That's the idea," Rogers says as he climbs back into a boat. "We want the French to think that the English army has landed and is surrounding the fort."

When the men finish setting up the fake camp, some stay there. You and the rest climb into the boats and head back to camp. It's almost dawn, so you crawl into your tent to get some sleep before the battle starts.

➸ *Turn to page 71.*

You and Jeremiah eat a meal of roasted chicken and fresh bread in one of the taverns. Then you get a room upstairs for the night.

It's around midnight when you wake up with a full bladder. The privy is in the courtyard outside. As you walk through the tavern, two men rise and follow you out.

"What's a young spit like you doing here?" one of the men hisses.

"Why, I think he's a rich gentleman with plenty of money for good food and drink," the other says. When you try to push past them, they knock you down. You hit your head and fall to the floor, unconscious.

When you wake up, it's morning. Jeremiah is standing over you. There's blood on your shirt.

"We've got to get to the ship!" you yell.

"The ship is gone," Jeremiah says sadly. "I guess you're not responsible enough for a job after all. Father has left for the war, so I have to take you home."

That's not fair! You beg your brother to change his mind, but he won't listen. As you ride away, you glance back and wish things had been different. Maybe you can come back next year.

THE END

To follow another path, turn to page 11.
To read the conclusion, turn to page 101.

Dropping the bait bucket, you run to the railing and pull at the line. Whatever is on the other end of the line pulls back. The force jerks you forward. You try to grab something, but it's too late. You are flung overboard!

The icy water feels like knives on your skin. You try to swim, but the current and the choppy waves pull you down. A huge codfish swims past you, a hook and line hanging out of its mouth. You wonder if it's the fish you tried to catch. It's the last thing you ever see as you drown in the cold ocean.

THE END

To follow another path, turn to page 11.
To read the conclusion, turn to page 101.

During the next few days, the pain in your hand gets worse. You try wrapping it in a clean cloth, but it doesn't help. By the fourth day you are flushed with fever and can't stand the pain any longer. Jeremiah unwraps your hand. You both are shocked—your skin is bright red, with pus oozing out of the wound.

By evening you fall unconscious. Soon your hand turns black. Gangrene! You are still unconscious when Skipper John and two sharesmen cut off your hand. They hope the operation will save you. But it's too late. You die there on the ship, never to see your parents or the farm again.

65

THE END

To follow another path, turn to page 11.
To read the conclusion, turn to page 101.

"Yes, sir," you say gratefully. "I hoped you'd hire me again."

Skipper John smiles at you. "You're a hard worker, and pretty tough to boot."

Jeremiah and the other crewmembers are glad to see you. You feel a little guilty about not returning to the farm, but maybe Adam can hire one of your neighbors to help.

You can't wait to go back to sea. If you work hard, you could become a sharesman like your brother. Maybe someday you could even become captain of your own fishing boat. Either way, the fishing life is for you.

THE END

To follow another path, turn to page 11.
To read the conclusion, turn to page 101.

66

"Thank you, skipper," you say politely. "But now that my father is gone to war, my mother and brother need me on the farm." Skipper John smiles and shakes your hand. Then he hands you some coins.

"A bit extra for your trouble," he says. "You're a good fisherman. If you decide to come back, you've got a berth on my boat."

You gratefully accept the money. It will help keep the farm going while Father is gone. Slowly you ride out of town, thankful that you survived.

THE END

To follow another path, turn to page 11.
To read the conclusion, turn to page 101.

You walk into the shadows carrying your musket. Suddenly you trip over a tree root and stumble into a large figure. You look up at his painted face and long black hair. It's the last thing you see as the Indian strikes you on the head with a tomahawk. You fall to the ground and die a few minutes later.

American Indians fought the British during the war.

THE END

To follow another path, turn to page 11.
To read the conclusion, turn to page 101.

You grab a saw and swim to the nearest log. Cutting the wood is slow work, and you tire quickly. The saw slips, and you feel a sharp pain in your leg. You keep going until the log is cut apart. As you swim to the next log, you feel light-headed and dizzy. A Ranger named Benjamin grabs you. You see a dark shadow in the water. You're horrified to realize that it's your blood.

"My word, man, you've cut your leg!" Benjamin cries.

"I know," you reply, "But it's not that bad. I can keep working."

"Let's take a look," Benjamin says.

Turn the page.

Two other Rangers grab you and haul you into the nearest boat. The cut isn't that deep, but the blood is still flowing freely.

"That's not good," Benjamin says. Another man takes off his shirt and tears a long strip of cloth off the bottom. The men use the cloth and a thick stick to tie a tourniquet above the cut. The bleeding slows, but you're having trouble breathing. Darkness closes in as you shut your eyes for the last time. You'll never know how the war ends.

70

THE END

To follow another path, turn to page 11.
To read the conclusion, turn to page 101.

The next morning the artillery is in place on the shores of Lake George. French cannons fire at you. Just as the British are to return fire, the French cannons fall silent.

Boom! A huge explosion rocks the fort.

"Did we shoot?" you ask, confused.

"No, the French are trying to destroy the fort from the inside," Father replies. He points to several canoes and boats rowing away from the fort across the lake. "Look, they're retreating."

"Shouldn't we chase them?" you ask.

Father smiles. "We don't care about the soldiers," he says. "All we want is the fort. And they've given it to us!"

Turn the page.

Explosions shake the fort for hours. You wonder if it will be destroyed. By the next day the explosions have stopped. The army enters the fort to put out the flames. The fort was heavily damaged, but it is still standing. General Amherst claims it for Britain. Its new name is Fort Ticonderoga.

The rebuilt Fort Ticonderoga is now a national park.

The army stays at the fort for some time. When General Amherst gives the order to move, Father comes to you.

"My term of service is finished," he says. "I'm going home. The general says you can go with me if you like."

You think about it for a minute. "No, I think I'll stay."

Father nods. The next day he leaves, and you prepare to march. You're not sure what will happen next, but you know that you like the life of a soldier.

73

THE END

To follow another path, turn to page 11.
To read the conclusion, turn to page 101.

Angry colonists protested British taxes and laws.

CHAPTER 4

Revolution in the Air

The sun streams through the open door of your father's Philadelphia tavern. It's 1774 and everyone seems to be complaining about something. For years the British and the colonists have grown increasingly angry at one another. The colonists feel that Britain's King George III doesn't care about them.

The Boston Tea Party sparked much of this anger. Last December a group of colonists dumped crates of tea into the Boston Harbor in the Massachusetts Colony. The colonists were protesting a British tax on the tea. The British Parliament then passed several harsh laws to punish the colonists. Now everyone wonders what's going to happen next.

Turn the page.

As you work, the noon crowd arrives. Your older brother Alexander works alongside Father, pouring mugs of ale. You're only 13, but you can serve food and drinks to the customers. The talk turns to the laws that many people call the Intolerable Acts.

"I can't believe the British closed Boston Harbor," one man says. "And they're trying to make Boston pay for the ruined tea!"

"But did you hear that several people tried to pay for the tea, and the British rejected the offer!" another replies.

"Then there's the Quartering Act," a stout man fumes. "The law says that British soldiers can stay in any home they want, for free!"

"Don't forget the Justice Act," another man pipes up. "It lets British soldiers who've committed crimes here be sent to England for trial. Of course they're going to be set free there. If the British can do that to Massachusetts, how long will it be before they can do it to the rest of the colonies?"

You look at your father. His lips are pressed tightly together. Father is loyal to King George, but he won't say anything to his customers that would hurt his business.

Father calls to you. He hands you a bundle wrapped in paper.

"Take this lunch to your Uncle Richard," he says. "He's building a house on Chestnut Street."

Turn the page.

As you turn to leave, a man sitting near the door motions to you.

"I'm Edward Biddle," the man says. He hands you a folded piece of paper and a shilling coin. "Can you take this message to the City Tavern? It's for a friend of mine, Paul Revere."

You gasp. "You know Paul Revere?" you stammer, impressed that he knows one of the most famous men in the colonies.

Biddle chuckles. "Yes, my boy, he's a fine man," he says. "Will you do my errand?"

"Of course!" you reply.

➤ To go to Chestnut Street first, go to page **79**.

➤ To deliver Biddle's message first, turn to page **80**.

There is much construction on Chestnut Street. On one side is Carpenters' Hall. Uncle Richard, a carpenter, is working down the street.

"Many thanks to your father," Uncle Richard says as he sits down for lunch. He spies the message in your hand. "Who is that for?" he asks.

"Mr. Edward Biddle gave me it to deliver to Paul Revere!" you tell him.

"Ah," Uncle Richard says. "Does your father know about that?"

"No," you say. "He doesn't like Mr. Revere and the other patriots. What do you think?"

"I can see both sides," Uncle Richard says. "Revere is a good man, though. You'd better not keep him waiting for his message."

You nod and head to the City Tavern.

Turn the page.

The City Tavern is the most important tavern in town, even though it was just built last year. The bartender tells you where you can find Paul Revere. He's relaxing in the coffee room. You bow and give Revere the message. He thanks you and hands you a coin.

"Excuse me, Mr. Revere?" you ask shyly.

He smiles. "Yes?"

"You were the talk of my father's inn," you say in a rush. "You rode into Philadelphia to bring the news that the British had closed Boston Harbor!"

"I'm glad the talk was good, then!" he says, laughing. Then he becomes serious. "Tell your father's customers that we will need many colonists on our side to resist the British and their unfair laws."

Paul Revere was famous as a silversmith and a patriot.

You nod, still in awe of the famous man. You know your father wouldn't approve of what Revere just said, though. Quickly you bow again and leave.

Turn the page.

It's late afternoon when you return to the tavern. Father is sitting with a man you recognize.

"Hello, Mr. Bradford," you say. William Bradford is a well-known printer in town. He's also a fierce American patriot.

"Your father says you are interested in learning the printing trade," Bradford tells you. "I'm willing for you to serve as an apprentice at my shop. At the end of seven years, you'll be a journeyman printer."

"I don't agree with your politics," Father tells Bradford. "Although I don't always like what the British are doing, I am a loyal Englishman."

"You're right, sir, we don't agree," Bradford says politely. "But this is about your son's future. Your older son will inherit the tavern, but what will become of this boy? I can give him an honest profession."

Father looks at you. "You do need to learn a trade. But I still could use your help in the tavern. It's up to you."

William Bradford published many articles against the British.

→ *To apprentice to Mr. Bradford, turn to page* **84**.

→ *To stay with Father, turn to page* **92**.

Bradford hands your father a contract to sign. In the contract you agree to an apprenticeship of seven years, to "serve your master faithfully, keep his secrets, obey his commands, and do no damage."

You won't earn wages, but Bradford will provide you with food, clothing, and a place to stay. The contract says that he will teach you math and reading. Plus, he will give you two new suits of clothing when your apprenticeship is completed.

Bradford takes you to his print shop. It is in the same building as his other business, the London Coffee House. Two other apprentices are at work, printing copies of the *Pennsylvania Journal*. They are much older than you and almost finished with their apprenticeships.

You settle into your new duties. You clean the shop, make sure there is plenty of ink for the printing press, and run errands.

The older apprentices, Thomas and Jacob, either ignore you or rudely order you around. It makes you angry to be treated this way. Mr. Bradford doesn't seem to notice.

You've had enough. One evening you sneak into Thomas and Jacob's small bedroom. You have a small bottle of ink in your hand. If you poured it over their belongings, that would teach them a lesson!

85

➤ To decide not to pour the ink, turn to page **86**.

➤ To pour the ink, turn to page **93**.

As happy as it would make you to get revenge, you decide against it. You instead speak to Mr. Bradford. The mistreatment stops.

As you get to know Bradford better, he talks to you about the rebellion he's sure will come. His ideas are very different from your father's, but you have to admit that they make some sense.

"I am a member of a group called the Sons of Liberty," he says to you one afternoon. "We're meeting tonight at the City Tavern. Would you like to come?"

➤ *To go to the meeting, go to page 87.*

➤ *To stay home, turn to page 95.*

Before you leave Bradford hands you a stack of pamphlets. "I want the other Sons of Liberty to send these to the other colonies," he says. "Many people are unhappy with the British. I want them to know they're not alone."

When you arrive at the City Tavern, Bradford goes inside, taking most of the pamphlets with him. "Take the rest to Benjamin Franklin's house," he tells you. "And don't let any Loyalists see them!"

You speed through the dark streets. As you turn a corner, you see three men in the street. You try to cross the street, but they block your way. "What's the hurry, boy?" one asks. You smell rum on his breath.

➤ *To stay where you are, turn to page **88**.*

➤ *To run, turn to page **96**.*

Thinking quickly, you stop. "Please forgive me," you plead. "My mother is sick, and I must find my father. He's in the City Tavern."

"Better get him, then," one man says. "Loyalists are going to raid the tavern tonight. All the traitors there will be clapped in irons."

You nod and run back to Bradford to tell him what is about to happen. Quickly the Sons of Liberty leave the tavern. You and Bradford return safely to the shop.

"I'm sorry I didn't deliver the pamphlets," you say, pulling the crumpled papers from your coat.

"You showed great courage tonight," Bradford says proudly. "You're a true Son of Liberty now."

By August the tension in the city is so strong that you can almost feel it. Word comes that in September there will be a big meeting in Philadelphia called the Continental Congress. Delegates from 12 of the 13 colonies will attend. Only the Georgia Colony isn't sending anyone. One afternoon two men come into the London Coffee House to speak to Bradford.

"We are Continental Congress delegates from Pennsylvania," they say. One of the men smiles at you. "You were my messenger once," he says. "I'm Edward Biddle."

You remember the nice man who paid you a shilling to deliver a message. He introduces his friend, Joseph Galloway.

Turn the page.

"We know of your loyalty to our cause," Biddle says to Bradford. "We'd like you to become the official printer of the Continental Congress."

Bradford eagerly accepts. Biddle looks at you. "If your master doesn't mind, we could use your help at the meetings. The delegates will need boys to fetch drinks and run errands."

"I still need his help in the shop, but I can spare him for the cause of liberty," Bradford says. He turns to you. "What would you like to do?"

➤ *To stay in the shop, turn to page* **97**.

➤ *To help at the meeting, turn to page* **98**.

The First Continental Congress met at Carpenters' Hall.

As much as you would like to become an apprentice, you know Father and Alexander need you more. "I'll stay," you say. Bradford shakes your hand and wishes you luck before he leaves.

You stay busy in the tavern. Father teaches you to do the accounting. You also order supplies from the local merchants.

Many Philadelphians flee the city's heat in summer. It's the time for fevers and sickness. One day you feel feverish yourself. Father puts you to bed in the back room, but you get worse. The next day Alexander also comes down with the sickness. The doctor says you have yellow fever. You both die two days later, leaving your grieving father to run the tavern alone.

THE END

To follow another path, turn to page 11.
To read the conclusion, turn to page 101.

You pour the ink over their clothing, blankets, and possessions. That will teach them!

The next morning Bradford bellows your name. Thomas and Jacob are standing beside him, smirking.

"Did you do this?" Bradford yells, holding out the ruined things. You bow your head and nod.

Bradford turns to Thomas and Jacob. "I have seen how badly you treat this boy. It is my fault for not correcting you sooner. But my oversight is not an excuse for your cruelty. Ten lashes each should teach you better manners." The two slink away.

Turn the page.

Bradford then turns to you. "I understand why you did what you did, but that doesn't excuse you. I have to buy them new clothing, shoes, and bedding. You should have spoken to me first."

"Ten lashes," he continues. "But that's not all. I must release you from your apprenticeship. I can no longer trust you. Someday you might be worthy to apprentice to someone else. But not to me."

You hang your head in shame. Father will be furious. The punishment you receive here will be nothing compared to what you will get at home.

94

THE END

To follow another path, turn to page 11.
To read the conclusion, turn to page 101.

It's hard to say no to your master, but you tell him that you need to stay home and study instead.

When Bradford leaves, you follow him. The tavern is crowded with the Sons of Liberty. You hide underneath an open window and listen. Then you go to Father's tavern. You tell him about the meeting.

"My Loyalist friends will be very interested in this news," Father says. "Make sure to keep your eyes and ears open in the future."

As you walk back to the print shop, you feel a little guilty. Mr. Bradford has been so kind to you. But then you remember that he's a traitor to Britain. Your father is proud of you, and that's what matters.

THE END

To follow another path, turn to page 11.
To read the conclusion, turn to page 101.

You don't know if the men are Loyalists or patriots. But you don't want them to discover the pamphlets.

Without looking, you dart into the dark street to get away from the men. "Look out!" a voice screams. As you look up, you see a carriage bearing down upon you.

"Whoa! Whoa!" the carriage driver shouts at his horses, but they can't stop in time. As you are pulled under the carriage wheels, the pamphlets are still clutched in your hand. They're the last things you will ever see.

THE END

To follow another path, turn to page 11.
To read the conclusion, turn to page 101.

The following weeks are busy. Bradford is printing all the documents of the Continental Congress. You run around town ordering paper and ink. Bradford attends the meetings every day. He comes back filled with excitement.

The meetings end in late October, and the delegates leave Philadelphia. Bradford comes into the shop with a stack of papers. "This is the Declaration and Resolves," he says. "It will be sent to King George!"

As the sheets come off the press, you pick up one and begin to read. It says that colonists "are entitled to life, liberty, and property." You hope that soon the colonies will win their freedom from the British. You are grateful to be alive during this exciting time.

THE END

To follow another path, turn to page 11.
To read the conclusion, turn to page 101.

97

On September 5 you arrive at Carpenters' Hall. Throughout the morning you bring water to the delegates as they discuss and argue.

As the weeks go by, you get to know some of the delegates. Samuel Adams, the delegate from Massachusetts, talks a great deal. His cousin John is quieter, but a powerful speaker. George Washington, from Virginia, listens carefully and writes many notes.

When the meetings end in late October, there is a huge party at the City Tavern. More than 500 people are there, including you and Bradford.

"What will Britain think of all this?" you ask Bradford as you leave the party. "Will the king even listen?"

"How can he not?" Bradford replies. "We've gone too far to back down now."

Patrick Henry (center) spoke to the other congressional delegates.

You shiver with excitement and fear. You don't know what the coming months will bring, but you're sure life in the colonies will never be the same.

99

THE END

To follow another path, turn to page 11.
To read the conclusion, turn to page 101.

Tobacco was an important crop in the southern colonies.

The End of the Colonial Era

The colonial era began with a few brave settlers willing to face an unknown, wild land in a search for freedom. In many ways it ended the same—with a war fought by people willing to die for their freedom.

By the 1640s thousands of people had come to Virginia and Maryland in the south and to Massachusetts in the north. When the colonists in Jamestown, Virginia, began growing and selling tobacco in Europe, there wasn't enough labor to grow the crops.

To fill the labor shortage, wealthy landowners contracted indentured servants to come to the colonies. Once they served their contracts, the servants were given land and set free. This promise of land and freedom drew tens of thousands of Europeans to the colonies. By 1700 a large percentage of colonists had been indentured at one time.

Over time the system of indentured servants was replaced by slavery. Captured Africans were brought to the colonies to become servants and slaves. Soon slaves became much more in demand than indentured servants. Slaves were more expensive, but they would never be freed. Slavery was especially common in the southern colonies. The huge plantations there relied on slave labor. It would be more than 200 years before slavery was abolished in America.

Captured Africans
were brought to the
colonies as slaves.

The colonies grew and spread quickly in the 1700s. At first many American Indian tribes sought friendship with the colonists. But things grew hostile as more settlers arrived and claimed Indian lands.

The British and the French both claimed land in the colonies, and they fought over it. Some tribes joined the French to fight against Great Britain in the French and Indian War. The British Army won the war, forcing the French to give up most of their northern lands. The British quickly took revenge on the American Indians who had fought for the French. Most of them were killed or forced from their lands.

The British had won a long, costly war. They needed to raise money. The British government passed laws that raised prices and imposed taxes on the colonists. The colonists resisted. As each law was passed, colonists became angrier. By 1775 the British and the colonists were at war. When the colonists won the Revolutionary War in 1783, it was the end of the colonial era.

The colonial era holds a special meaning for Americans. During this time colonists began moving toward becoming an independent country. Today's ideals of freedom and self-reliance came from the courage and hard work of the settlers, servants, and slaves who first came to the colonies.

TIMELINE

1607—Jamestown Colony is founded in Virginia.

1614—The first tobacco is exported to Europe from Virginia.

1619—The first African servants are brought to Virginia.

1620—The ship *Mayflower* brings colonists to Plymouth, Massachusetts.

1634—Colonists arrive in Maryland and establish St. Mary's City.

1641—Sir William Berkeley becomes governor of the Virginia Colony.

1681—William Penn founds Pennsylvania.

1754—The French and Indian War begins.

1759—The British Army captures Fort Carillon from the French and renames it Fort Ticonderoga.

1760—George III becomes king of Great Britain.

1763—The French and Indian War ends.

1765—The Stamp Act is the first direct tax on the colonies by the British.

1770—The Boston Massacre occurs when five colonists are killed during a skirmish with British soldiers.

1773—The Boston Tea Party occurs.

1774—The British Parliament passes the Intolerable Acts to punish the colonists for the Boston Tea Party.

The First Continental Congress meets in Philadelphia and writes the Declaration and Resolves.

1775—The Second Continental Congress meets in Philadelphia.

George Washington is appointed chief of the new Continental Army.

April 19, 1775—The first battles of the Revolutionary War take place at Lexington and Concord, Massachusetts.

July 4, 1776—The Continental Congress adopts the Declaration of Independence.

1783—The United States wins the Revolutionary War and its independence.

OTHER PATHS TO EXPLORE

In this book you've seen how the events of the colonial era look different from three points of view. Perspectives on history are as varied as the people who lived it. Seeing history from many points of view is an important part of understanding it.

Here are some ideas for other colonial points of view to explore:

+ Many American Indian tribes lived throughout the lands that became the colonies. As more colonists came, the tribes were pushed off their lands. What would it have been like to be an American Indian watching these settlers pouring into your lands?

+ Many early colonists knew nothing about growing food, hunting, or building their own homes. Few brought tools or supplies with them. What were the first years in the colonies like for them?

+ British soldiers were stationed throughout the colonies. These men were far from home, with few friends. How would a young British soldier feel about living in such an unfriendly environment?

READ MORE

Fishkin, Rebecca Love. *English Colonies in America.*
Minneapolis: Compass Point Books, 2009.

McNeese, Tim. *Colonial America, 1543–1763.*
New York: Chelsea House, 2010.

Nardo, Don. *The Establishment of the Thirteen Colonies.*
Detroit: Lucent Books, 2010.

Raum, Elizabeth. *The Dreadful, Smelly Colonies: The
Disgusting Details about Life During Colonial America.*
Mankato, Minn.: Capstone Press, 2010.

INTERNET SITES

FactHound offers a safe, fun way to find Internet sites
related to this book. All of the sites on FactHound have
been researched by our staff.

Here's all you do:
Visit *www.facthound.com*
Type in this code: 9781429654814

GLOSSARY

cauterize (KAH-tuh-rize)—to brand a wound with a hot iron

curtsy (KURT-see)—to bend slightly at the knee, with one leg crossed behind the other; colonial women curtsied as a sign of respect

fugitive (FYOO-juh-tiv)—a person who runs away, especially from the law or justice

gangrene (GANG-green)—a condition that occurs when flesh decays

Loyalist (LOI-uh-list)—a colonist who was loyal to Great Britain during the Revolutionary War

militia (muh-LISH-uh)—a group of citizens who are trained to fight but only serve in time of emergency

musket (MUHSS-kit)—a type of gun with a long barrel

pamphlet (PAM-flit)—a small printed booklet

poultice (POLL-tuhss)—a soft substance applied to wounds

tourniquet (TUR-nuh-ket)—a tight wrapping designed to prevent a major loss of blood from a wound

traitor (TRAY-tuhr)—someone who turns against his or her country

Bibliography

Ballagh, James Curtis. *White Servitude in the Colony of Virginia: A Study of the System of Indentured Labor in the American Colonies.* New York: Burt Franklin, 1969.

Cressy, David. *Coming Over: Migration and Communication between England and New England in the Seventeenth Century.* New York: Cambridge University Press, 1987.

Earle, Alice Morse. *Home Life in Colonial Days.* Stockbridge, Mass.: Berkshire House Publishers, 1992.

Fox, Christopher. *"Without a Single Shot:" The 1759 "Siege" of Fort Ticonderoga.* 20 Oct. 2010. www.fort-ticonderoga.org/history/online-resources/articles/1759-fort-ticonderoga-seige.pdf

Green Spring Plantation: A Historical Survey. 20 Oct. 2010. www.historicgreenspring.org/plantation_history.php

Leckie, Robert. *A Few Acres of Snow: The Saga of the French and Indian Wars.* New York: J. Wiley and Sons, 1999.

Magra, Christopher. *New England Cod Fishing Industry and Maritime Dimensions of the American Revolution.* PhD dissertation, University of Pittsburgh, 2006. 20 Oct. 2010. http://etd.library.pitt.edu/ETD/available/etd-05312006-104527/unrestricted/Magra_ETD_1_.pdf

INDEX